Rabbits

The Ultimate Beginner's Guide to Raising Healthy Rabbits for Life!

D1462194

Karen Sutterin Copyright © 2015

Table of Contents

Introduction

I want to thank you and congratulate you for downloading the book, "Rabbits - The Ultimate Beginner's Guide to Raising Healthy Rabbits for Life!"

This book contains proven steps and strategies for raising healthy and wonderful rabbits! These sociable, lovable animals are easy to love however, they are not quite easy to raise and care for.

This book will teach you the specific requirements and care they need. Make them your wonderful companions by taking time to learn what kind of diet, habitat, hygiene and health treatments suit them. Considering taking care of a rabbit requires knowledge and that's what this book offers.

If you take the time to read this book fully and apply the information held within, this book will help you to become a better and responsible rabbit owner. Be equipped with tips, strategies and helpful information about rabbit care. Know the dos and don'ts to avoid harming them. Most of all learn the benefits a rabbit can bring to you and the rest of the family.

Like domestic cats and dogs, rabbits are also fun and playful creatures. If you are deciding to have them at home or you already have one, let this book be your guide to raise them efficiently!

Thanks again for downloading this book, I hope you enjoy it!

Chapter 1

Understanding Rabbits as Pets

Like domestic cats and dogs, rabbits are also popular pets that every family can have. They are gentle animals, soft and relatively clean. There are various breeds to choose from depending on the characteristics and size you prefer. The most owned breeds are the Mini Lop and Dutch which are both good companions for kids with their social nature and smaller size.

Smaller breeds are usually 2-3 pounds while larger breeds such as the Flemish Giant may weigh up to 24 pounds and may grow up to 3 feet. Moreover, female rabbits or Does can live with each other harmoniously however; the male rabbits or Bucks tend to fight if caged together. Likewise, they should be kept away from dogs and cats but can be housed together with guinea pigs.

PERSONALITY

Primarily, rabbits are bred for their meat and fur. This maybe the reason why it is challenging to win the trust and loyalty of these tiny creatures compared to cats and dogs. Once in a while, you may encounter a rabbit aggressive and quiet hard to tame especially the larger breeds. However, they are highly sociable, intelligent and affectionate once you've won their "hearts". On the other hand, they can be also destructive, bratty, willful and vengeful but having the right knowledge will help you manage these complex animals.

Unfortunately, many of us adopt or purchase a rabbit without deeply understanding their nature and behavior. Likewise, most owners tend to dump their already matured rabbits when it is finally at its strongest personality.

MISCONCEPTIONS ON BUNNY HANDLING

The most usual misconception of people regarding rabbit is that it looks like plush toys, and that they prefer to be cuddled and held. Considering the rabbit's natural history, they are ground-dwelling species and serves as prey for most predators in the wild. Hence, it is against their natural tendency to be held above the ground. They feel helpless and out of control of their activities and actions.

However, this doesn't mean that you can never pick up or held your rabbit. Remember never pick them through their ears. Gently place one hand under its ribcage and the other hand, playing its rear end. Lift it quickly and turn it around where its feet are placed against the handler's chest. It will make the rabbit feel more safe and secure and is less likely to struggle.

TREATS WILL HELP

Giving your rabbit little treats such as banana, apple, carrot or oats may help you in taming it. Lie close on the ground and let it go out of its clutch or cage on its own. Never grab or force the rabbit to come near you or it might be harder for it to build trust.

Moreover, do not expect for your rabbit to immediately approach you. Be patient even if it takes hours to go to you. They are eventually shy but curious creatures so they are more likely to come over to look around and sniff you. Let them do this and resist the temptation of grabbing and petting them. Lastly, make it feel that he's free to move without being grabbed or touch and learn that there's no threat.

PLAYTIME

During playtime, allow your rabbit to lose its wariness on you by not touching it often. It should come gradually. Extending a hand or finger for him to sniff is an ideal start. It will more likely to allow you to touch its ears, back, temples or forehead. Be patient and do not force or chase your rabbit.

Even you consider your rabbit as family pet, only adult members should be its primary care provider. Children can play with them but should not be left alone or the rabbit's safety will be at stake. Teach the kids in the household how to properly take care of the rabbit as well as the dos and don'ts in handling them.

Chapter 2

A Safe and Secure Place to Live

Adding a domestic rabbit in the family is likewise, adding a new member to it. One of the most essential decisions to make is where to place your rabbit's habitat. You must ensure that it has a safe and secure place to live.

Are you putting it indoor or outdoor? Basically domestic rabbits should be keeping indoors since they cannot tolerate hot weather and extreme temperatures that their wild relatives can endure. Moreover, they are highly at risk from predators when they are outside. Believe it or not, they can suffer from heart attack and die with just the mere sound and sight of a wild animal nearby. However, if there is no way you can keep it indoors, make sure that the area is fully covered and protected.

Indoors or Outdoors

Letting your bunny indoors will lead you to the next question: Will you let it roam freely around the house? If yes, ensure that the house or that certain area where it will live is free from electrical wires. Remember, they like to chew and nibble on something so keep all the cords out of reach and cover the outlets to prevent injuries and premature death.

Likewise, chewing can lead to poisoning if substances, chemicals and other objects are left open. Aside from the common toxins and substances such as rodenticides, cleaning supplies, insecticides, and perfumes, plants like calla lily, azalea, aloe and Lily of the Valley can be poisonous to them.

If you decided to put it in a cage, the cage must be spacious enough for the rabbit to move around easily. It should be at least five time the rabbit's size. It should also be able to stand up on its hind legs and stretch out without bumping its head on the cage. Whilst wire is an ideal material to use in making a cage or clutch, avoid using it for flooring as it can harm the rabbit's feet and cause injuries. Their feet are sensitive since it does not have protective pads like that of the cats and dogs. If you will use wood, keep it at a minimum as rabbits tend to nibble on it.

Furthermore, the cage should be away from direct sunlight and predators. Keep it in a shady place if outside because they can get sick with the extreme heat. Avoid putting its clutch or cage in humid areas such as attics, bathrooms or basements. There is a huge tendency for molds to grow in these areas and molds can kill rabbits.

Areas that are high moisture must also be avoided as it increase respiratory issues among them and can cause premature death. Moreover, natural light is also recommended for a rabbit's room however; do not put it in direct sunlight. Keep the room cool around 60F to 70F temperature to avoid heat stroke.

Place for Play

They usually sleep during daytime so you must respect their "quiet time". You can place a box made of cardboard inside the cage where they can hide comfortably. The rabbit also need to be out of the cage for a few hours every day to exercise. Rabbits enjoy jumping, running and roaming around their surroundings which is an ideal chance for you to interact and play with your rabbit. Just make sure that it has a safe and secured place to play.

The Litter Box

Rabbits have the ability to easily learn how to use the litter box like cats. To encourage this behavior, put a litter box inside its cage. If the rabbit is able to roam all over the house, it is best to put similar looking litter box in various places. Ensure that is of the right size since rabbits usually enjoy their time in the litter box. However, do not use wood shavings or cedar in the bedding as it can trigger allergic reactions or may cause liver damage to them.

Use organic litters and avoid dusty kitty litters as it can cause health problems to them. Choose litters that are made of citrus, wood pulp or paper. You can also use newspaper but it is not as absorbent as the other materials. Likewise, put some fresh hay every day in the litter box so they have something to snack on while staying there.

Chapter 3

Balanced Diet for Rabbits

Like human, animals also require a proper, balanced diet to protect them from serious illnesses and to be overall fit. However, rabbits are known to have complex digestive systems. Most of the problems and health issues associated with them are due to poor diet and incompatible foods. Basically, a rabbit's diet should be composed of the following foods;

VEGETABLES- this is one of their basic diets and must be composed of green, leafy vegetables like romaine lettuces, cilantro, parsley, collard greens and dandelion greens. Feed them with at least three different varieties of veggies every meal. You can introduce new vegetables by trying to add it one at a time in smaller amounts. Root vegetables and dark green leafy vegetables are highly recommended for feeding. Do not feed it with rhubarb and beans.

HAY- rabbits must have a constant supply of hay, specifically, the Timothy grass hay. It helps them digest their foods and gives them the necessary fiber to fight certain health problems such as obesity, hair balls and diarrhea. For adult rabbits, Alfalfa hay can be given but only in limited amount as it is very rich. This is high in calcium, calories and proteins.

FRUITS- aside from vegetables and hay, rabbits also love fruits and other treats. Papaya, apples minus its seeds, pears, blueberries, melon, peaches and plums are great treats for them. Avoid giving extra-sugary fruits and treats more often like banana and raisins.

PELLETS- while fresh foods are ideal for rabbits, some still choose to feed them with pellets. It is available in several formulas and brands, containing the necessary nutrients for a rabbit. Ask for the assistance if you are purchasing pellets to know the right feed for your pet. Find out the proper portioning of the feeds depending on the size, breed and situation of the rabbit. For lactating or pregnant rabbits, you can give them unlimited food.

Pellets should only be given as supplement and not as substitute to fresh foods. Feed the rabbit in moderation and only choose pellets that are Timothy-based. Other manufacturers include corn, seeds and other high-calorie ingredients in rabbit feed which is not healthy for them.

Likewise, make sure that the pellets are fresh and relatively rich in fiber. It should be given less as the rabbit grows older.

WATER- is also one of the most essential things in a rabbit's daily diet. They cannot acquire water from the foods they eat unlike humans so they should be frequently provided with fresh, clean water every day.

Make sure that the food dish you are using is heavy enough to avoid food spill. Likewise, the water dish or container should also be heavy enough and can hold plenty of water. Make this equipment always sanitize and clean to avoid diseases. Moreover, with the rabbit's sensitive digestion, there are certain foods that you should feed to them. These include tomatoes, iceberg lettuce, corn, cabbage, beans, potatoes, peas, onions, beets, bamboo seeds, rhubarb and grains. Also, avoid giving them candy, chocolates or sugary foods. Ask your vet first before introducing new foods to them.

Something to Chew

Chewing is a natural behavior of a rabbit. To keep them chewing without damaging things in the house and exposing them to risk, put some cardboard or untreated woods in their cage. Paper-towel rolls and other chewable materials that can be easily disposed are also ideal. Avoid giving those sharp objects or those who has soft rubber and loose parts. If you have the extra budget, there are inexpensive materials meant for rabbit's chewing that are available in the market and online that you can try.

Food Portions

For baby rabbits, the mother's milk is best from birth up to 3 weeks. On its 4th week, you can incorporate alfalfa and pellets to its diet with mother's milk. Introduce hay on its 7 weeks onwards and vegetables on its 12th week. For rabbits that are 7 months and older, oat hay, timothy hay and grass hay can be given and reduce the amount of pellets. For fruits, give your rabbit not more than 2 oz per 6 pounds of its body weight.

Mature rabbits (1 to 5 years old) can be given with unlimited supply of hays and Bermuda grass. The quantity of pellets should be ¼ cup to ½ cup per 6 pounds of the rabbit's body weight or proportion to vegetables. Slowly introduce greens and veggies to avoid digestive problems.

For rabbits over 6 years (senior), you can continue the adult diet if the rabbit is healthy and maintain its ideal weight. If the rabbit is underweight, give it more pellets to gain the necessary weight.

Chapter 4

Grooming and Hygiene

Rabbits are meticulous in terms of cleanliness. They spend more time grooming and cleaning themselves. Whilst they do not require regular baths, regular brushing is a needed to keep their fur shiny and in good condition. This will also prevent hair balls. One must be extra careful when grooming them since they are very delicate animals. Below are the basics in grooming your rabbit safely.

Shedding

Rabbits usually shed every 3 months. Alternately, they will experience light shedding which is barely noticeable and heavy shedding which is natural. Since they are meticulous groomers, rabbits insist on keeping themselves tidy and clean by licking themselves like cats do. This causes hairballs, a health problem due to ingesting large quantities of hair. Unfortunately, they cannot vomit unlike cats so they have a tendency to develop giant masses of hair tangled with food which blocks their stomach.

Brushing

Short-haired rabbits must be brushed at least once a week. During the heavy shedding period, it is ideal to brush them daily. Remember that their skin is quite delicate and fragile so be careful in using a brush. Avoid metal tooth brushes and choose bristle brush designed for them. After brushing, run a damp washcloth on its coat.

This weekly brushing will remove loose hair and helps the rabbit's coat prepare in the succeeding multiple brushing sessions for their heavy shedding period. They shed differently so expect your pet to shed in a couple of weeks or more. Remove the loose hair immediately or the rabbit will do it. If you notice some bald spots during heavy shedding, don't fret. It will grow back within a couple of week.

Long-haired rabbits required more attention in terms of grooming compared to other short-haired breeds. Keep their fur neat by regularly trimming them to an inch and to avoid hair balls. It is advisable to consult a veterinary first before doing the above tasks.

Bathing

Vast majority of the rabbit's breeds do not enjoy getting wet. Although there are rare cases where a rabbit grow up near ponds, lakes or swimming pools, they are similar with cats that do not relish water. Likewise, an occasional bath can still be stressful to an average bunny thus, it is not recommended.

Unless required by your veterinary let's say to cool down its fever, never bath your sick rabbit. It may only compromise his health and behavior. There are other safe options to control fleas aside from bathing.

Moreover, a wet rabbit will take a long time to dry thus, spot cleaning is ideal. Rabbits are also prone to hypothermia so make sure to blow dry its hair thoroughly when it gets wet for any reason. Their normal body temperature is ranging from 101 – 103 degree Fahrenheit so make sure that the blow dry setting is not higher than "warm". Use baby cornstarch and not talcum in grooming them. The latter is carcinogenic and might harm the rabbit. Use a flea comb and gently comb out the dirt.

Skin care

Rabbits have delicate skin and they are vulnerable to cuts. Use a mat rake or mat splitter instead of cutting the mat with scissors. Usually, bald patches and flaky skin is a sign of mites or an allergic reaction due to fleas. Consult a veterinarian first before using anti-flea products.

Feet

Regular trimming is required especially if the house rabbit spends most of its time in linoleum and carpets at home. However, declawing is not advisable to avoid the risk of infection. Place a large box of hay and straw to address the rabbit's excessive scratching and digging activities. Also, provide rugs or resting pads if the rabbit's feet padding (fur) is worn down, have callused skin or has inflamed. Keep litter boxes dry as well to prevent an exposed skin from being urine burned and infected.

Scent Glands

The rabbit's scent glands can be found under its chin and around the anus. This is the reason why they chin things and people so as mark to them. If there is an unpleasant odor coming from the anus, it is most likely due to scent glands build up.

Using a q-tip dipped in warm water, gently clean the rabbit's genitals while holding it safely. Find the two slits on the sides of its genitals and carefully swab away the buildup.

Ears

Use a cotton swab to lift ear wax but be careful not to push it down the canal. You can try using mild ear cleaner. If there's ear mite infestation, consult your vet for topical medications available. Likewise, a smelly ear or having puss on them is a sign of infection. Take your rabbit to your vet for remedies.

Teeth

The rabbit's teeth continuously grow. It must be checked regularly to see if the tooth is wearing down accordingly. For rabbits with crooked teeth, trimming must be done with guillotine-type clippers. If left untreated, the rabbit couldn't be able to eat properly and may starve to death. Ask your veterinarian how to properly clip your rabbit's teeth.

Eyes

Watery or discharge from the eyes needs to be treated immediately. Aside from getting the proper medications and eye drops, the rabbit's check must be also kept clean and dry to prevent the peeling of fur or being chafed. You can use clean tissues to absorb the wetness. If there are painful lesions in the area, a prescribed anesthetic powder can be applied.

Nails

Like their teeth, the rabbit's nails grow continuously and can be very long and sharp. Light-colored nails are easier to trim however; the dark colored nails are quite difficult since the blood is not visible. Ask your vet to clip the nails of your rabbit if you are not comfortable to do it. It should be trimmed every 6 to 8 weeks.

Litter Training

Training rabbits that are three months below can be difficult since they are still too immature to learn and use the litter box consistently. Be patient if your bunny is not yet picking up the points of using the litter pan at first. Keep an eye on it whenever it is outside the cage. Notice that it's pushing its butt against an object or raising its tail, those are the signs that it is getting prepared to urinate. Put him back on the cage immediately to let him realize that he should have urinated. This trick will help your pet rabbit use the litter pan in no time. Choose a litter pan that is appropriate with your rabbit's size and age. Make sure that it can easily work on the litter pan and that it will fit in the rabbit's cage.

Whilst rabbits are fastidiously self-groomers, owners should still be responsible in grooming them. Moreover, grooming time is the ideal time to bond with your rabbit and get to know it deeply. Check him from head to toe and examine his genitals and overall body as these are good indicators when something is not right with him. Aside from grooming, check thoroughly for bumps, lumps, fleas or cuts and overgrown teeth and nails and treat it immediately.

Chapter 5

Getting Rid of the Fleas

Another common annoyance that a rabbit has to conquer all throughout its life is flea season. Fortunately, most of cat flea products are relatively safe to use to rabbits however, when the infestation is severe, the cure itself can be more stressful for the rabbit.

The Culprits

Fleas are tiny insects that feed on the blood of other animals or hosts. They are the carriers of certain diseases and infections. Rabbits are also prone to have fleas since the latter can fly and transfer from one animal to another. The fleas can thrive for a few months and their eggs can be usually found all over the households especially on carpets and animal beddings. Thus, ensure that these places are always clean and newly replace.

Unlike animals, humans are not really affected by fleas. They can only experience rashes in the wrists and ankles but only if the infestation is severe. Once the pets are treated, their owners do not need treatment and is no longer affected.

The Risk Factor

Fleas can jump from its host to another. The rabbit is usually affected by fleas when it comes in direct contact with the affected animal such as cats and dogs. They can also transmit fleas to other rabbits. Moreover, contaminated areas such as upholstery and carpets make it easier to transmit fleas.

Diagnosing Infestation

You cannot easily notice fleas on the rabbit's fur. The dirt or black spots you can see on its fur are usually the flea's feces. This is the symptom of infestation. The rabbit may scratch the affected areas or may chew its rear due to itching.

Keep in mind that rabbit fleas are normally found on its ears. During brushing session, check thoroughly if there are brown and black objects in the rabbit's fur. If left untreated, your pet can be anemic due to blood loss.

Products to Avoid

There were cases of death after using a flea dip or flea shampoo to treat the rabbit. However, it is still unknown the exact cause of death- the ingredient of the dip and shampoo or the stress of bathing- so it is recommended to avoid both. In most foster homes for the rabbits, room sprays were usually used to eliminate fleas. The rabbit should be kept out of the room to be sprayed for at least 24 hours. There are several products that are safe to use to get rid of the fleas and mites. However, there are also products to be avoided.

FLEA SHAMPOO- apparently, bathing the rabbit is not advisable due to numerous health reasons. It can also cause stress to them so it is strongly discouraged. Flea dips and baths are both a big no.

FRONTLINE- is another product that is unsafe to use to rabbits. Although it is safe to use in dogs and cats, it has been associated in neurological damage and even deaths among rabbits.

FLEA POWDERS- are only ideal for cats and dogs. Even the product says "rabbit safe"; experts still do not recommend using these products on rabbits.

The market is flourished with various flea products stating that it is rabbit safe but be extra cautious with these products. They may not be as effective and as safe as your vet's recommended treatments. Keep in mind that rabbits have very delicate immune systems and using inappropriate treatments can only aggravate their condition. Fine, flea comb is helpful in removing the fleas although this cannot totally eliminate them.

If the home has been infested with fleas, sprays can help to eradicate them. Also, isolate affected animals to prevent transmission to other animals. Regular cleaning, replacing the rabbit's beddings and sanitizing will greatly help to reduce fleas.

Chapter 6

Common Rabbit Diseases and Health Care

Rabbits are susceptible to a wide range of maladies and diseases. Some breeds are even more prone to inherited disorders compared to others. These diseases can affect their quality of life so as an owner, it is your responsibility to have your rabbit checked regularly by a veterinarian. Below are some of the most diseases or health conditions present in rabbits.

ABSCESS- is a bump on the rabbit's skin that is usually filled with pus. It is a symptom of serious infection that maybe a result of scratch or cut. Abscess can also be a manifestation of parasitic invasion also known as warbles.

BLOODY URINE- can be a symptom of urinary stones, bladder infection or uterine cancer in a rabbit. However, a condition called red urine where the rabbit's urine is orange or reddish in color but is not really blood.

CANCER- specifically, uterine cancer affects rabbits but other types are very seldom to affect them. The symptoms include weight loss, loss of appetite and lethargy.

COLDS- rabbits are also susceptible to colds, sinuses, runny nose and other conditions of the upper respiratory system. There are cases wherein a rabbit's cold is actually a disease known as snuffles.

DIARRHEA- a rabbit with diarrhea experiences frequent stool droppings or is jell-like. It can be due to coccidiosis or enteritis.

COCCIDIOSIS- is an infection of the gastrointestinal tract. Diarrhea can lead to dehydration, liver damage, weight loss and poor weight gain.

ENTERITIS- bacterial infection can cause inflammation in the rabbit's intestine which is called enteritis. Among the symptoms are diarrhea, lack of appetite, lethargy and painful abdomen. This condition that is known to cause by E. Coli can make a rabbit weaken, dehydrated and slows down its digestive system.

EAR MITE- similar with fleas, ear mites are parasites that can mainly found in the rabbit's ear. You can notice it when your rabbit shakes its head frequently and scratches its ears often. Severe cases include red and sore ear with discharge.

FLY STRIKE-is another infestation of tiny insects such as maggots or fly larvae in the rabbit's skin. An open sore or areas of the skin dampened with urine or feces are where these flies usually lay their eggs. Once burrowed in the rabbit's flesh, they produce toxins causing state of shock to its hosts. The symptoms include itchiness, listlessness, irritated skin and in severe cases, seizures.

HAIR BALLS- as discussed earlier, rabbits are groomer which is why during shedding; they groom themselves by licking loose hair. These hair buildups known as hairballs or wool block obstruct the rabbit's digestive system and stop the gut movements.

HEATSTROKE- extremely hot weather can cause heatstroke among rabbits. The overheated rabbit will experience panting, wet nose and sweating. The nose will turn blue in extreme cases. Younger rabbits, long-haired rabbits and the seniors are the most susceptible to heat stroke.

PIN WORMS- are worm-like parasites that usually infest the rabbit's ceacum and large intestines. The pinworms can be seen around the anus or on its droppings. It can result to weight loss or difficulty in gaining weight. Likewise, this condition can be transmitted and contagious among rabbits.

RUNNY EYES- is the continuously tearing of an eye or both which can be a sign of other illness. It can be also due to irritation by strong substances or chemicals, blockage in tear duct, allergy, bacterial infection, injury or due to heredity.

VHD- or Viral Hemorrhagic Disease is an infectious viral disease which attacks the rabbit's internal organs specifically the liver. Most likely, the infected rabbit can die within 24 hours because of the massive hemorrhage of its internal organs. The symptoms include muscles spasms, lethargy, and congestion, loss of appetite, fever and bleeding. The disease is prevalent in China, New Zealand and other European countries.

VENT INFECTION- is an infection of the rabbit's "vent" region on its genitals. Small pustules can take form which can burst. The condition is said to be due to urine nibbles or dirt that are not totally cleaned off. Moreover, the infection can be transmitted through mating.

WRY NECK OR HEADTILT- is a common condition in which the head of the rabbit tilts to other side and the chine tilts to the opposite side. The common causes of head tilt are ear infection, trauma to the head, damaging the inner ear, stroke and tumors.

Prevention and Cure

A balanced, healthy diet is still one of the best ways to prevent your rabbit from acquiring most of the diseases mentioned above. Ask your trusted vet on safe rabbit supplements and how it can help boost your pet's health. Moreover, only use medicines and treatments prescribe by a veterinarian to avoid negative side effects and aggravating the condition. Make it a habit to check your rabbit's body and examine if there are symptoms of possible illnesses.

If your rabbit is eating more often or barely eats, most likely that it is in pain or ill. The frequency of droppings, changes in its drinking and eating habits are also strong indications that it could be seriously sick. Stress is also a contributing factor to make them ill so check its environment and look for possible stressors such as other animals or pets in the household and children. Enthusiastic kids can also stress the rabbits by constantly handling, picking and chasing them incorrectly.

Keep the Environment Clean

Flea, mite and other infestation of parasites can be address by thorough cleaning. Check the litter boxes and beddings regularly to see if they are need to be refreshed or totally cleaned. Ensure that the surface hay is always dry and dump the soiled litter properly. Wash and air dry the litter boxes. You can use vinegar for disinfection and brush it if necessary.

Vaccinations

Fortunately, there are available vaccines to help boost your rabbit's health and resistance to certain diseases. These will also aid in stimulating the production of antibodies for their immunity. Moreover, getting your rabbit vaccinated will help you acquire him pet insurance since most companies required vaccinations as proof of medical record.

Neutering

Usually, rabbits that haven't been spayed or neutered spray urine. This is their way of marking territories. If you don't have plans of breeding it, have it neutered to prevent this problem. Likewise, this will also keep them from unnecessary multiplying.

Quarantine

If you own several pair of bunnies at home, it is not advisable to separate those pairs who are bonded since it can add stress on them. Assuming that the sick bunny's companion is already exposed and affected, you can set up a mini quarantine. Minimize also their shared spaces by creating partitions among their clutches or cages.

Changes in Behavior

Rabbits that are injured, ill or in pain mostly act strangely which you can use in determining the possible problems. They feel pain like humans and other mammals do so be sure to always have it checked. Your vet can provide symptom checker to help you find out your pet's illness and the appropriate treatments.

As responsible pet owners, we are all required to ensure that our pets including domestic or house rabbits are in good shape. Likewise, make sure that they are safe, protected from injuries diseases and suffering. Provide your rabbit with proper medical care such as annual check-ups. Also, prefer a veterinarian that has experience in treating rabbits since not all of these vets are able to treat them. Look for nearby clinics in case of an emergency.

Conclusion

Thank you again for downloading this book!

I hope this book was able to help you to learn and understand the things to consider, requirements, dos and don'ts and essential information when having a house or pet rabbit.

The next step is to abide all the rabbit rules, follow the tips in raising them and implement other advice discussed in this book to become a responsible rabbit owner.

Whilst rabbits are not like the traditional household pets (like cats and dogs) they too can become a loyal, friendly and charming family member provided that you show love, affection and care for them. They are complex but sociable and gentle creatures that require supervision and a great deal of understanding as well. They also have special needs that we must attend to. Sooner all your efforts as a rabbit owner will be paid off with these animal's companionship, enjoyment and even profits!

Let this book be your reminder of how to raise healthy rabbits. Moreover, share the knowledge you acquire and teach others on how to treat rabbits properly.

Finally, if you enjoyed this book, please take the time to share your thoughts and post a review on Amazon. It'd be greatly appreciated!

Thank you and good luck!

Bonus Chapter: If You Love Rabbits Consider a Guinea Pig

Guinea pigs can be such lovely pets. They are small, cute and actually quite comical. They are wonderful creatures and they can easily provide entertainment for people of all ages. If they are cared for properly, they can be very tame. Once you win their hearts, you can easily treat them as lap pets. They'll happily munch on food as you stroke their hair. Some guinea pigs who receive proper care live for as long as six to ten years!

Typically, guinea pigs are considered as pets for children. Since they are so small, many assume that taking care of guinea pigs is easy. However, there are many things to consider if you want to raise guinea pigs. It's still a responsibility that you need to prepare for in any way you can.

It's important to keep in mind that guinea pigs are not toys.

Regardless of how small guinea pigs seem to be, they need constant care and attention from a responsible adult who can provide them with their needs. Children should never be allowed to care for guinea pigs without supervision. Guinea pigs are delicate creatures. They can appear fragile and nervous if they are unhappy in their environment. If they are uncomfortable, they might jump off when being handled. When they are suffering from a lot of stress, there's a good chance that they'll get hurt or injured. Before buying a guinea pig, you should first learn about their basic needs in order to ensure that your pets would receive the best kind of care.

Scientifically speaking, guinea pigs don't come from Guinea, nor are they considered pigs. They are from the species *Cavia Porcellus* from the family *Rodentia,* and they are believed to have originated from South America. There is a popular theory that they are called "pigs" because they grunt and squeal like pigs. "Guinea", an old English coin, was the price of a guinea pig when it was sold by British sailors in the 1600's. Hence the name "guinea pigs".

Do you think that guinea pigs are the right pets for you? Are you ready to give them attention and long-term commitment?

Here are some of the advantages of owning and caring for guinea pigs.

They are friendly and sociable

When tamed and cared for properly, guinea pigs can be extremely docile. They rare bite and they are very sociable creatures. Guinea pigs love interaction with other guinea pigs or with humans. In fact, a guinea pig with no companion is very likely to die easily. They have a "herd" mentality which always makes them seek companionship. Their natural instinct to gather and be with others is what makes them such pleasant pets.

They can be easily petted and trained. Given the proper stimulation, they can even be trained to do tricks! Since they are used to companionship, it is a bad idea to keep them in an isolated area of your home. Always make sure that you put them in a location where they can interact with the other members of the family. It would be best if you can get at least two guinea pigs so that they have each other a companions.

They are easy to care for

Perhaps many older children are given the responsibility to care for guinea pigs because they are considered easy to care for. All they need are the basics and they will survive. You don't need to buy a lot of equipment and you don't need a big space. Since they are small, they require little maintenance.

Generally speaking, all they need are fresh water, timothy hay, dry pellets and vegetables. Many owners invest in cages in order to give guinea pigs a controlled environment, but even their cages only need to be cleaned about once every two weeks. They shouldn't be bathed more than twice a year. Also, vet costs are often very low. The only regular grooming they need is clipping of nails once every three weeks.

They don't usually cause trouble

It can be such a pain to care for pets who can be destructive. Some really wild ones can even end up destroying your house! With guinea pigs, you don't have this problem. They are really small, so you can't expect them to create a lot of damage. It's not in their nature to bite or tear up our carpet. They are just too small, too fragile, too nervous and slow to create this kind of damage.

The greatest damage that they can do is pee and poop around your home. However, this can still be prevented by making sure that their territory is limited to a cage or to a small and controlled area. Some guinea pig owners claim that they have successfully litter trained their guinea pigs, but these cases are very rare.

Guinea pigs are not expensive

In general, pets are expensive to maintain. It's almost similar to having another child in your home. They have needs, and as the owner, it is your responsibility to provide.

If you are looking for an option that won't burn a hole in your pocket, guinea pigs are perhaps the best option for you. You don't even have to buy them! You can adopt guinea pigs from a shelter. There are a lot of guinea pigs who are looking for a home. Most shelters will even be willing to teach you how to care for your guinea pigs upon adoption.

Perhaps the only thing that would really cost you when buying guinea pigs is setting up their home. You'd have to invest in a cage and buy beddings. If you are really determined to save money, you can even opt to just make your own cage. This is ideal because you can customize the size and adjust the materials according to what will be most convenient for you. You also have to invest in beddings for your guinea pig's home. If you have extra cash, you can buy wood shavings for your guinea pigs. But as always, there are cheaper options, if you want something more affordable, you can invest in fleece instead.

As long as your guinea pigs don't get really sick, you won't really spend much on veterinarian visits. Also, food pellets are pretty affordable so you don't have to worry about feeding them. Once you settle them in their home and get their routines fixed, you won't need to shell out a significant amount of cash anymore.

They live long

For such small creatures, the life span of guinea pigs is pretty long. The average lifespan of guinea pigs is about four to six years, but if you give them first-class care, they might live for up to ten years! For comparison, rats and hamsters can live for only an average of about two to three years.

Also, even if they look small, nervous and fragile, they are not as sickly as other small pets. It's very unlikely that you'll suddenly find them sick dead. Overall, guinea pigs have stable lives. You don't need to constantly worry about their health and well-being.

Preparing for your guinea pig

Do you think that you are ready to buy or adopt guinea pigs anytime soon? Before you head to the pet store or adoption shelter, you must first prepare yourself for the responsibilities of owning a guinea pig. As the pet owner, it is going to be your responsibility to provide the guinea pigs with all their red such as food, grooming, exercise, and general care.

Here are some of the things that you should consider before bringing in a guinea pig into your home.

Check for allergies. It is a definite possibility for you and your loved ones to be allergic to guinea pigs. Before you commit to adopt or buy guinea pigs, you first have to make sure that you won't have any bad reactions when exposed to these creatures. It is also a good idea to check if you are allergic bedding materials like fleece, hay or wood shavings.

If you have small children living in your home, it is also a good idea to brief them about the guinea pigs. It is important for them to understand the responsibilities of having a guinea pig around. Children who don't understand the importance of taking care of a pet may subject the creature to torture without realizing it. It's important to give them an idea on how to care for the pet in the right way.

One of the most important things to do in order to avoid problems is to keep the living area of your guinea pigs clean and hygienic. Even if guinea pigs are relatively small pets, it is still important to make sure that their urine and droppings are cleaned often. This will ensure that you won't encounter health problems that can cause problems for you, your pet and your family. Keeping pig quarters clean means trying to develop a regular routine which will help you get rid of unwanted substances in the living area of your guinea pig. As you get to know your pet better, you will find it easier to figure out what routine works for you and your pet.

Read up on what possible health issues you should expect when raising guinea pigs so that you'll be able to take necessary steps to avoid health problems for you and your family. By knowing the possible health issues you can encounter in the future, you can prevent your guinea pig from acquiring various illnesses.

For example, one of the things that you should watch out for is obesity. Guinea pigs tend to eat a lot and gain excess weight. It is a good idea to control their food and to allow them to exercise for a few hours a day in order to ensure that their bodies won't balloon. There are also other things to watch out for like heat stroke, lung problems and dental problems. Keep in mind that you also have to ensure that they get good grooming. Constantly brush their fur to avoid mites and lice. Also, make sure to constantly trim their nails.

Made in the USA
Monee, IL
30 November 2019